薩卡加維亞

Heroes and Role Models | Non-Fiction Series

Copyright © 2022 by Level Learning, INC. and Washington Yu Ying PCS™
Original and Edited Text Copyright © 2022 by Washington Yu Ying PCS™

All rights reserved. No part of this book in whole or part may be reproduced without written permission from the publisher.

Published by Level Learning, INC.

Content Contributors:
Washington Yu Ying PCS™
Level Learning - Ya-Ching Chang

Illustrations by: Josh Taira

Leveling classification based on Level Learning standard. For full description, visit www.levellearning.com

ISBN 978-1-64040-038-2
Traditional Chinese Edition

About Level Learning:
Level Learning provides a literacy focused curriculum specifically designed for K-12 Chinese as a Second Language classrooms. Our program offers 20 levels of specific and detailed objectives, leveled texts and passages, mastery-based online assessment, and analytics to enable data-driven instruction. Level Learning reading curriculum for both literature and informational text emphasize grammar and comprehension skills to help teachers develop confident and independent Chinese language readers. The non-fiction series of books are specifically designed to support our informational text course based on multiple national standards. To learn more about our entire offering, visit www.levellearning.com.

About Washington Yu Ying PCS™:
Washington Yu Ying PCS is a Mandarin English dual language immersion International Baccalaureate (IB) World school. Yu Ying's mission is to inspire and prepare young people to create a better world by challenging them to reach their full potential in a nurturing Chinese/English educational environment. Yu Ying's comprehensive IB, dual immersion curriculum equips students with global competencies for success in the real world. As a leader in immersion education, Yu Ying is determined to advance Chinese language programs and global citizenry education by helping other schools create and strengthen their Chinese programs. For more information, email: products@washingtonyuying.org

你知道薩卡加維亞的故事嗎？薩卡加維亞出生於1788年。她是美國原住民，也是一位著名的遠征者。

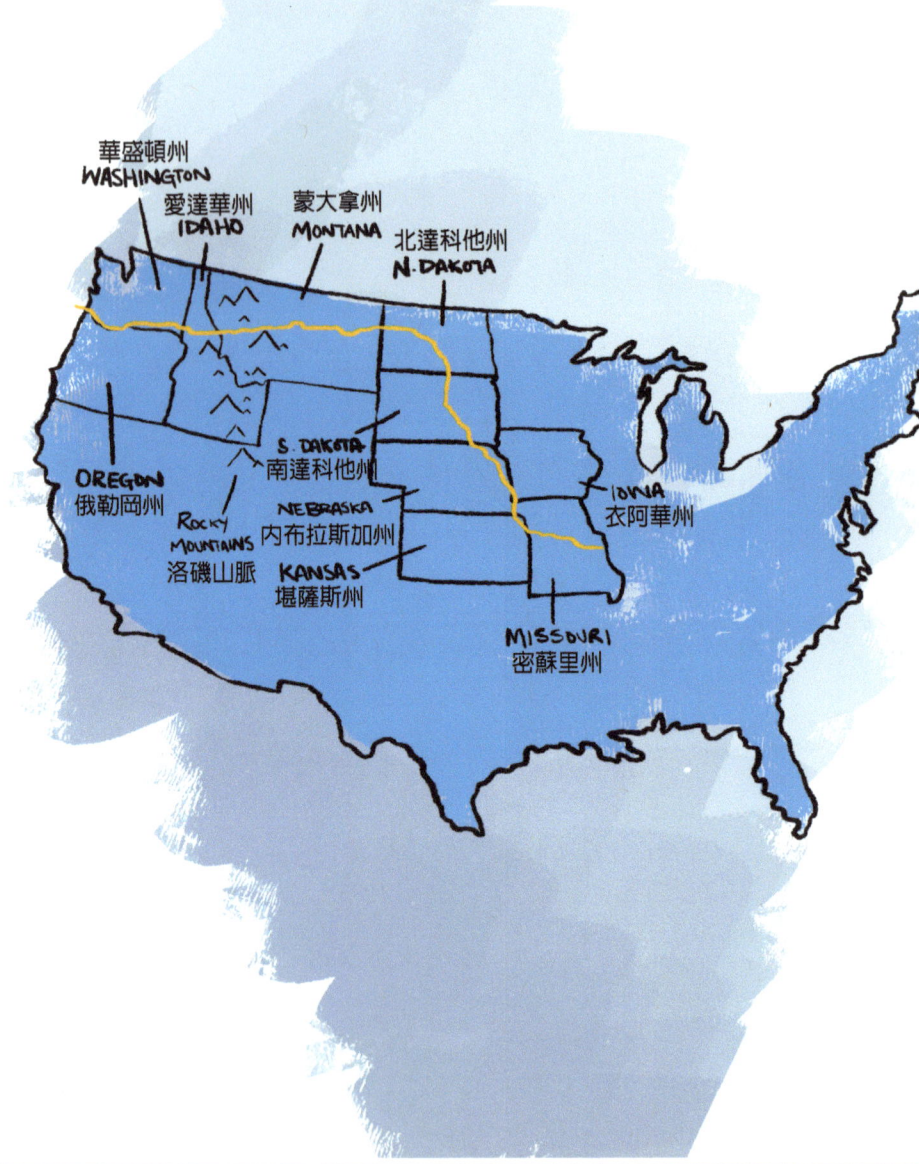

有一天，薩卡加維亞住的村子裡來了一支遠征隊。路易斯和克拉克帶著這支遠征隊，想要前往美國西部。因為他們不會說原住民語，所以需要村民的幫助。

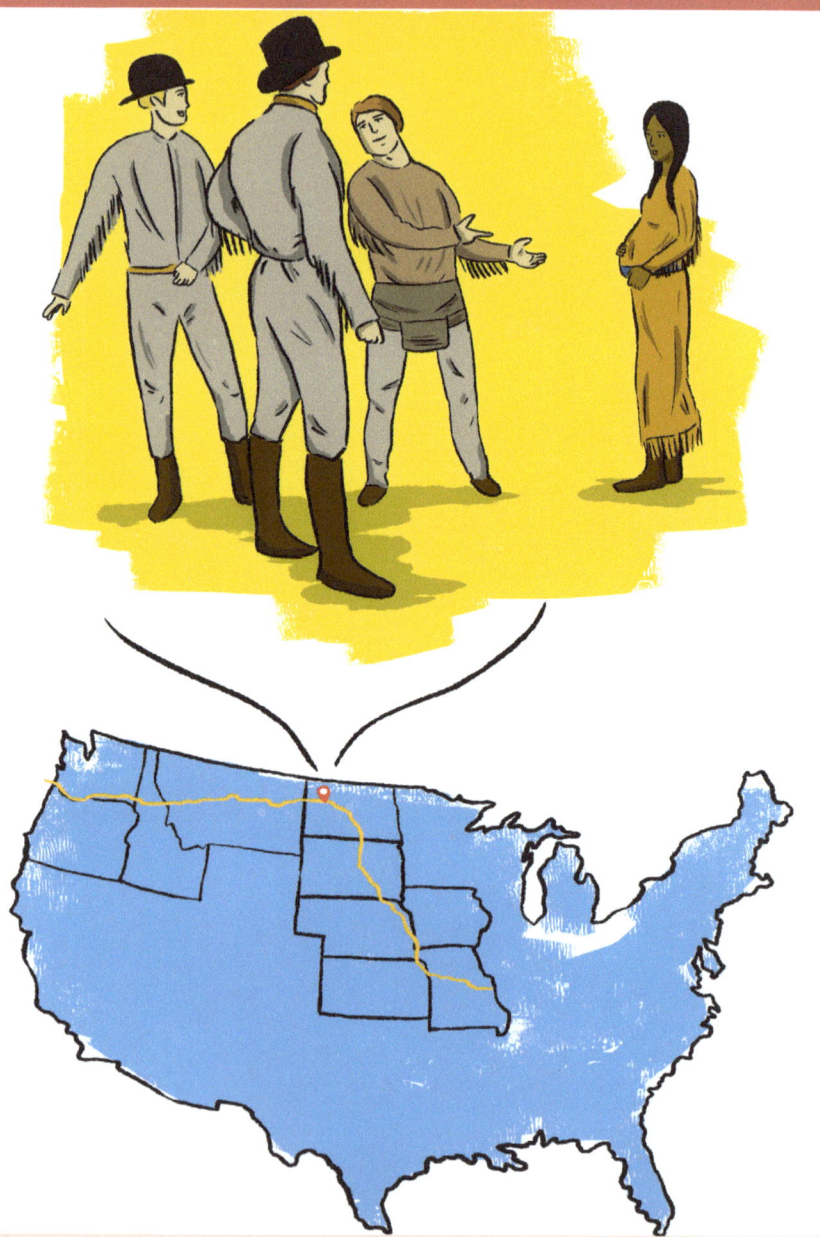

薩卡加維亞會說原住民語。路易斯和克拉克知道以後,希望她可以加入遠征隊。那時候,懷孕的薩卡加維亞快要生寶寶了。

不久後，薩卡加維亞就生下了一個寶寶。為了幫助路易斯和克拉克，她便帶著寶寶加入了遠征隊。

前往西部的路上，天氣非常寒冷。大家經常又冷又餓，沒有東西吃。薩卡加維亞教大家採集可以吃的植物和果實。

除此之外，薩卡加維亞還幫忙帶路和翻譯。路上的原住民看到了女人和寶寶，都對遠征隊非常友善。路易斯和克拉克相信薩卡加維亞和寶寶為大家帶來了和平。

有了薩卡加維亞的幫助，這次的遠征非常順利。遠征隊到達了美國西部，也見到了太平洋。

在2000年，美國發行了一枚新的硬幣。硬幣上有薩卡加維亞帶寶寶遠征的畫像。這枚硬幣是用來紀念薩卡加維亞對遠征的幫助。

Glossary

	Pinyin	English Definition
原住民	yuán zhù mín	natives
著名	zhù míng	famous
村子	cūn zi	village
遠征隊	yuǎn zhēng duì	expedition team
前往	qián wǎng	to go
西部	xī bù	west
原住民語	yuán zhù mín yǔ	native language
需要	xū yào	to need
村民	cūn mín	villagers
幫助	bāng zhù	help
加入	jiā rù	to join
懷孕	huái yùn	pregnant
寒冷	hán lěng	cold
採集	cǎi jí	to collect, to gather
植物	zhí wù	plant

	Pinyin	English Definition
果實	guǒ shí	fruit
帶路	dài lù	to guide the way
翻譯	fān yì	to translate
友善	yǒu shàn	friendly
相信	xiāng xìn	believe
和平	hé píng	peace
順利	shùn lì	smoothly
到達	dào dá	to reach, to arrive
太平洋	tài píng yáng	Pacific Ocean
發行	fā xíng	to issue
硬幣	yìng bì	coin
畫像	huà xiàng	portrait
紀念	jì niàn	to commemorate, to remember

www.ingramcontent.com/pod-product-compliance
Lightning Source LLC
Chambersburg PA
CBHW041225070526
44584CB00001B/98